DISCARD
Sonia Sotomayor

An Introduction to the Prospective
Supreme Court Justice

Margarita Amador

Cover design by M.A.
Cover background photo: U.S. Supreme Court
Back cover photo: Pete Souza, White House, 5/29/09

Seattle, Washington, United States of America

10 9 8 7 6 5 4 3 2 1

ISBN   1448602483
           9781448602483

"In view of the Constitution, in the eye of the law, there is in this country no superior, dominant, ruling class of citizens. There is no caste here. Our Constitution is colorblind, and neither knows nor tolerates classes among citizens."

Justice John Marshall Harlan, dissenting
Plessy v. Ferguson, 1896

Introduction

Sonia Sotomayor is the first Hispanic woman to be nominated to the Supreme Court of the United States. The Bronx-born Puerto Rican is an embodiment of the American Dream, working hard since childhood to rise from poverty to wealth and influence. With a strong Democratic majority in the Senate, she should easily be confirmed as a Supreme Court Justice.

Sotomayor was mentioned as a prospective justice for decades before her nomination. In 1995, a lawyer was quoted in the *Boston Herald* describing Sotomayor as "someone with a bright future with aspirations to become the first Hispanic on the Supreme Court."[1] In the late 1990s when she was nominated to the 2nd Circuit Court of Appeals by President Clinton, many speculated Clinton wanted to appoint her to the Supreme Court before he left office. Fearing this prospect, Republicans blocked her confirmation for over a year.

Conservative Rush Limbaugh warned she was an ultraliberal on a "rocket ship" to the high court.[2] After her confirmation, reporters hounded her with questions of her potential Supreme Court aspirations.[3] In 2004, her name appeared frequently in articles speculating on Supreme Court nominees. Insiders hinted she could be nominated by either presidential candidate, Kerry or Bush.[4]

On May 1, 2009, the stage was set for Sotomayor. Associate Justice David Souter announced he would be retiring from the Supreme Court. Sotomayor was cited by numerous groups as a potential replacement. President Obama said he would look for someone with empathy, "someone who understands that justice isn't about some abstract legal theory or footnote in a casebook. It is also about how our laws affect the daily realities of people's lives."[5] On May 26, he announced Sonia Sotomayor as his nominee. Sources close the White House said Obama's team wanted a person who could win over Justice Anthony Kennedy, a centrist on the Court, with clear and well-reasoned arguments.[6]

Sotomayor was immediately embroiled in controversy following her nomination. Racially charged comments from her past were circulated online and in the news, including one where she said she hoped a Latina woman would judge better than a white male. Her detractors labeled her a racist who would unjustly side with minorities if permitted a seat on the Supreme Court. Past rulings were scrutinized to show she was a judicial activist who legislated from the bench. Democrats only added to the racial drama, with White House Press Secretary Robert Gibbs telling Republicans to be "exceedingly careful" in the way they criticized the Latina nominee.[7]

Given the initial excitement, many have warned that a contentious confirmation process may lie ahead for the nominee. However, the outcry over Sotomayor's alleged racism or judicial activism could quickly dissipate. With a government ruled almost entirely by one party, objections from Republicans and Independents are irrelevant. Sotomayor should easily be confirmed. Fearing charges of racism, Republicans will most likely remain tepid in their opposition. Tabloider Arianna Huffington advised her readers during the first flurry of controversy, "it's going to be a total snooze."[8]

Still, Republicans might find it worthwhile to attack Sotomayor for political gain as they prepare for the 2010 elections. Columnist Charles Krauthammer recommends they refute her but then vote to confirm:

> Make the case for individual vs. group rights, for justice vs. empathy. Then vote to confirm Sotomayor *solely* on the grounds – consistently violated by the Democrats, including Sen. Obama – that a president is entitled to deference on his Supreme Court nominees, particularly one who so thoroughly reflects the mainstream views of the winning party. Elections have consequences.[9]

Republicans will, most likely, vote to approve Sotomayor regardless of the debate. They are too fearful of losing the Hispanic vote in their respective districts to vote against her.

So, who is the woman well-positioned to become the next Supreme Court Justice? Where did she come from and how did she reach this point in her career? Most importantly, what does she believe, and what might Americans expect from her as a judge? The following is an overview of her inspiring life story, a record of some of her major decisions as a judge, and a brief sample of the dramatic controversy which has accompanied her nomination.

On Her Way to the Top

Sonia Sotomayor was born June 25, 1954, in the Bronx. Her parents moved to New York City from Puerto Rico during World War II. Her father was a tool-and-die worker from the Santurce area of San Juan, while her mother was raised in the neighborhood of Santa Rosa in Lajas, a rural area on the island's southwest coast. Sotomayor has one sibling, a younger brother named Juan. The family remained closely connected to Puerto Rico after leaving for New York, and to this day Sotomayor visits aunts, cousins, and other extended family on the island once or twice per year.[10]

Sotomayor represents a true rags to riches story. She grew up in a public housing project in the Bronx. Her health was poor, and at age 8 she was diagnosed with diabetes. She has taken insulin shots ever since. English was rarely used in her home, as her father, who had the equivalent of a third grade education, spoke only Spanish.

She didn't become motivated to master English until the age of 9 when, tragically, her father died.[11]

Everything changed in the family as her mother, Celina, was left to raise her children almost entirely on her own. She provided for them by working six days a week as a nurse. Celina was adamant her children would work hard, receive excellent educations, and pull themselves up to better circumstances. Sotomayor says of her mother, "I saw her working, being the emotional and spiritual leader in our family... She had almost a fanatical emphasis on education. We got encyclopedias, and she struggled to make those payments. She kept saying, 'I don't care what you do, but be the best at it.'"[12] Sotomayor recalls they were the only family in the neighborhood to actually buy the encyclopedias from the salesman. Her mother paid for her and her brother to attend Catholic school. Though often away working, she always kept a warm pot of rice and beans on the stovetop for the kids and their friends.[13]

Sotomayor decided at an early age she would one day become a judge. Her first career goal was to be a sort of Puerto Rican Nancy Drew, but those dreams were dashed when she was diagnosed with diabetes. Doctors suggested that given her poor health, she might pick a more "sedate career." Shortly after, she saw an episode of *Perry Mason* in which a prosecutor said he didn't mind losing a case if the defendant was innocent because that meant justice was served. Sotomayor recalls, "I thought, what a wonderful occupation to have… And I made the quantum leap: If that was the prosecutor's job, then the guy who made the decision to dismiss the case was the judge."[14] She realized the judge "was the most important person in the room."[15] Her mind was made up: "that was what I was going to be."[16]

Though the projects in the Bronx were far from an ideal setting for the aspiring judge, they gave her an unusual motivation to succeed. As drugs increasingly became an issue, Sotomayor broke from her peers and devoted herself to her studies. She remembers seeing drug dealers lurking in the halls of her building, and addicts strung out in the streets. She was strongly impacted by the desperation of the people around her:

> There were working poor in the projects. There were poor poor in the projects. There were sick poor in the projects. There were addicts and nonaddicts and all sorts of people, every one of them with problems, and each group with a different response, different methods of survival, different reactions to the adversity they were facing," she said. "And you saw kids making choices.[17]

Sotomayor commuted five miles to Cardinal Spellman High School, a well-respected, middle-class Catholic school. She served on student government and was active in the forensics club, which required memorizing and delivering long speeches. She was diligent in her studies, and ultimately graduated class valedictorian in 1972.[18]

Her hard work paid off. After graduating high school, she was admitted to Princeton University. She felt like "a visitor landing in an alien country" when she arrived at the elitist school. Sotomayor was so uncomfortable her first year, she never raised her hand in class. She was "too embarrassed and too intimidated to ask questions."[19] Still, she performed better than most of her classmates, earning the premier academic award, the Pyne Prize, and graduating summa cum laude with a degree in history. Next to her yearbook photo she listed a quote by socialist Norman Thomas: "I am not a champion of lost causes, but of causes not yet won."[20]

From Princeton, Sotomayor enrolled in Yale Law School. She continued to excel in class and was an editor of the Yale Law Journal. While there, she published a note on the possibility of Puerto Rican statehood.[21] She married Kevin Edward Noonan while in school, but divorced shortly after without any children.[22]

Sotomayor first made national headlines during her final year at Yale Law

School. She went to a recruiting dinner with the Washington law firm Shaw, Pittman, Potts & Trowbridge. One of the firm's partners asked her questions focusing on her Puerto Rican heritage. According to Sotomayor, the questions were along the lines of: "Do law firms do a disservice by hiring minority students who the firms know do not have the necessary credentials and will then fire in three to four years? Would [you] have been admitted to the law school if [you] were not a Puerto Rican? [Were you] culturally deprived?" The next day she confronted the recruiter during a formal interview. He was surprised to learn he caused any offense and apologized to Sotomayor, inviting her to attend further interviews. Sotomayor declined and instead filed a formal complaint against the law firm. A Yale student-faculty tribunal demanded the firm issue an official apology. They did, but the tribunal found it unsatisfactory: "the firm did not seem fully to recognize the consequences of its partner's action." The firm then wrote another, more penitent letter, which the tribunal found adequate. If the firm had not appeased the offended groups, it would have been barred from recruiting at Yale.[23]

The incident arose from Sotomayor's discomfort in the elite circles in which she found herself. She said in a speech much later in life, "I have spent my years since Princeton, while at law school and in my various professional jobs, not feeling completely a part of the worlds I inhabit… I am always looking over my shoulder wondering if I measure up."[24]

After college, Sotomayor spent five years as a prosecutor with the Manhattan District Attorney, where colleagues remember her zeal for pursuing cases of pedophilia and child pornography.[25] She also served on the board of the Puerto Rican Legal Defense and Education Fund. She was devoted to her work, and ultimately received a big-salary offer from a midtown Manhattan law firm, Pavia & Harcourt.

Sotomayor proved herself in the world of commercial litigation. A 1992 *New York Times* article describes the firm: "The views from Pavia & Harcourt's 12th-floor offices in midtown Manhattan are commanding, and the carpeted halls, in soft pastels, are adorned by modern Italian paintings."[26] She spent eight years with Pavia & Harcourt, eventually becoming a partner in the firm.[27]

Though private practice provided a hefty paycheck, Sotomayor always intended to return to the public sector. She maintained her childhood dream of one day becoming a judge. In 1992, she finally got her chance. She was recommended for the federal bench by Senator Daniel Patrick Moynihan, a New York Democrat. Moynihan had a deal with his Republican counterpart, Senator Alfonse M. D'Amato, to share district court judge selections in New York.[28] So, despite Sotomayor's liberal leaning, President George H.W. Bush heeded Moynihan's recommendation and nominated her to the court.

Judge Sonia Sotomayor

On October 2, 1992, Sotomayor took the oath for a seat on the Federal court of the Southern District of New York, covering Manhattan, the Bronx, and six upstate counties. She was the first Hispanic American to be seated on the federal bench in Manhattan.[29] At the time of her nomination, Hispanics comprised about 13% of the state of New York and 25% of New York City, but there were no Hispanic judges on the federal bench.[30]

In Sotomayor's first year, the liberal Alliance for Justice gave her the highest rating of any Bush appointee. She ruled on a wide variety of cases during her first appointment to the court. In January, 1993, she ordered that a photocopy of a torn up note found in the briefcase of former White House Counsel Vincent Foster be made available to the public. Foster had committed suicide and the government said the note could not be released because of his family's privacy concerns.[31]

In September, 1993, she ruled on a case involving the Hell's Angels. The government attempted to seize a Manhattan building owned by the Hell's Angels motorcycle club because it was allegedly linked to cocaine and methamphetamine sales. The building was said, moreover, to promote "criminality and the unconventional lifestyle of its members." Sotomayor said the government's evidence was "rather scanty indeed." She let the Hell's Angels keep the building.[32]

Sotomayor defended religious expression in December, 1993, striking down a White Plains, New York, law prohibiting the public display of religious or political symbols in the city's parks. Sotomayor ruled the law was unconstitutional. In May, 1994, she ordered prison officials in New York to allow two inmates to wear Santeria religion beads under their belts.[33]

Sotomayor's biggest case to date came in 1995 when, many say, she "saved the sport of baseball," ending a 232 day strike by baseball players. The teams' owners had negotiated a salary cap which the players' union rejected. The sport grinded to a halt, with the 1994 World Series and subsequent games cancelled. In January, 1995, Congress introduced multiple bills attempting to end the strike, but to no avail. President Clinton ordered the two sides reach an agreement by February 6. The deadline passed and Clinton was ignored. The following month, all eyes turned to Judge Sonia Sotomayor, who scheduled a hearing to intervene. Sotomayor acknowledged, "I know nothing about this except what a common lay person reads in the New York Times."[34] She urged the groups to reach a conclusion on their own: "I suspect the public would like you to resolve it without our intervention."[35]

The players made it known they would end their strike if Sotomayor granted an injunction against the owners, allowing the players to return under the 1994 work rules.[36] President Clinton issued a statement indicating what all parties involved – including Judge Sotomayor – should do:

"players have agreed to return to work if the District Court judge issues an injunction. If the judge does grant the injunction, I hope the owners decide to let the players play ball."[37] The *Boston Herald* encouraged fans to expect a quick decision from the judge: "Like Roger Clemens, Sotomayor is apparently inclined to work quickly when she has the ball."[38]

On April 1, Sotomayor issued the injunction only 15 minutes after hearing the case. She ordered the owners to restore the provisions of the expired agreement. Sotomayor opined, "This strike has placed the entire concept of collective bargaining on trial."[39] The *Fort Worth Star-Telegram* reported she "chided baseball owners, saying they have no right to unilaterally eliminate the 20-year-old system of free agents and salary arbitration while bargaining continues." According to the *Chicago Tribune,* she "took the bat out of the hands of the owners, who had appeared to be winning the dispute, and put it firmly in the hands of the players ."[40] The owners appealed their case in the 2nd Circuit Court of Appeals, but the panel upheld Sotomayor's ruling.[41]

The reaction to her decision was mixed. Many felt she had overstepped her bounds.[42] They were bothered by her hasty ruling, as if the owners' arguments had been irrelevant, and the light manner in which she dispensed with the case, quipping "I probably would have liked more time to practice my swing."[43] The *Chicago Sun-Times* reported, "Her ruling was even more of a 'victory' for players than they had hoped. And it was more of a 'loss' for the owners than their lawyers had dreamed."[44] In other words, it was more heavy-handed than anyone expected. Still, she ended a nearly eight month disagreement to which there was no end in sight, and her ruling was upheld by the Court of Appeals.

Sotomayor has dealt with abortion-related issues only a few times as a judge. On one such occasion in 1996, she issued an injunction against four protesters from coming within 15 feet of an abortion clinic, the Women's Medical Pavilion, in Dobbs

Ferry, New York. She upheld a 1994 ruling mandating open access to abortion clinics.[45]

In 1997, Sotomayor heard a dispute between publishers and freelance writers. Publishers wanted to archive freelance stories online without paying additional fees to the authors. Sotomayor ruled in favor of the publishers, explaining "while 'modern developments' have changed the financial landscape in publishing, copyright laws written more than three decades ago still gave publishers a broad right to recreate their publications in electronic form." Sotomayor told the freelance writers if they wanted copyright laws changed, they should look to Congress rather than the courts.[46] Her ruling was reversed two years later.[47]

In March, 1998, Sotomayor penalized a business coalition for luring homeless people to do work in return for "job training" and pay of only $1 per hour. She ordered the coalition to pay back wages, overtime, and lawyers' fees to the workers.[48] The settlement amounted to $816,000 total for 198 people, of which about $400,000 was distributed to 70 people two years later.[49]

In October, 1998, Sotomayor moved one step closer to the Supreme Court. She was confirmed by the Senate to a seat on the 2nd Circuit Court of Appeals in a 68-28 vote. Her confirmation was stalled for months by skeptical Republicans who feared her future aspirations.[50]

The most notable case from Sotomayor's time on the 2nd Circuit Court of Appeals, and the one most likely to cause debate during her confirmation, is *Ricci v. DeStefano*. The 2003 case deals with racial discrimination on the part of the New Haven Fire Department. The department administered a series of tests to determine a new set of lieutenants and captains. The tests were carefully constructed by an independent party to avoid racial bias. After a great deal of studying, including investment in studying materials, seventeen whites and one Hispanic scored high enough to obtain the promotions. The city threw the tests out because no blacks performed well enough to merit the promotion. Ricci and the other white firefighters sued DeStefano, the mayor, claiming reverse racial discrimination. They lost in federal court and then lost again in the 2nd Circuit Court of Appeals. Sotomayor sided against the white firefighters. The case is expected to go to the Supreme Court.[51]

Many have identified the case as proof Sotomayor is a judicial activist who favors minorities over the majority. The ruling is, appropriately, receiving a great deal of scrutiny, and could very well be reversed in the Supreme Court. However, columnist Eugene Robinson argues her decision was not about racial identity or activism, but about following the law:

> What Sotomayor's attackers either don't understand or won't acknowledge is that the issue before the court wasn't whether the city of New Haven had acted fairly in canceling the exam, but whether it had acted legally. There was ample precedent indicating that the action was, in fact, legal. I thought the whole theory of judicial restraint was that we didn't want unelected judges telling our elected officials what to do. I

thought the conservative idea was that judges were just supposed to 'call balls and strikes' -- which is just what Sotomayor and her colleagues did.[52]

Other notable cases from the past decade include:

- October, 2001: Sotomayor ruled that a dyslexic woman who had failed the bar exam five times in an attempt to become a lawyer should be allowed extra time, a computer, and a large-print version of the exam.[53]

- September, 2002: In *Center for Reproductive Law and Policy v. Bush*, Sotomayor upheld the Bush administration's Mexico City Policy, which required federally funded NGO's to refrain from performing or promoting abortion services in foreign countries. Sotomayor said "the government is free to favor the anti-abortion position over the pro-choice position, and can do so with public funds."[54]

- September, 2003: Sotomayor approved police "perp walks," a punishment in which "handcuffed, camera-shy defendants are paraded before cameras" so as to "sway others from attempting crimes similar to those charged to the defendants."[55]

- January, 2004: Sotomayor ruled against the Bush administration in its attempts to scale back energy efficiency standards. She said the change would have violated an energy law passed by Congress in 1975 and amended in 1987. The Bush administration said the tough standards would make air conditioners more costly.[56]

- March, 2008: Sotomayor supported a decision limiting the free speech rights of a high school student. The student, Avery Doninger, posted negative comments about school administrators on her personal blog and subsequently was removed from her position as senior class secretary. The question was whether a school could limit students' speech off campus, and the extent to which the Internet might blur the boundaries of a "school campus." Sotomayor was skeptical of the administrators' action, saying "pedagogical rights can't supersede the rights of students off campus to have First Amendment rights."[57] However, she ultimately sided with the school officials.[58]

Overall, Sotomayor does not appear to be the ideologue some might fear or hope for. The majority of her rulings are well-defended. Nonetheless, critics point to a few disturbing cases and comments which might call into question her aptitude for the high court. I turn now to the major issues she will face in the confirmation process.

The Empathetic Latina: Should Justice Be Blind or Biased?

Sotomayor is hailed as the first Hispanic American nominated to the Supreme Court. The designation is actually a bit hazy, as Benjamin Cardozo, who served on the Supreme Court from 1932 to 1938, was a Jew of Portuguese heritage.[59] Nonetheless, Sotomayor's nomination is touted as a milestone for Hispanic Americans. She is presented not so much as an individual, but as a symbol for a large and growing segment of the population.

The significance of the event is not lost on Sotomayor. Her ethnicity is central to her identity. She readily admits to seeing the world in racial terms. Reflecting on her time as an assistant district attorney, she says "[the] saddest crimes for me were the ones that my own people committed against each other."[60] Her tribal worldview was undoubtedly ingrained in her by her family and Puerto Rican community. Upon hearing news of her nomination to the Supreme Court, a resident of her mother's ancestral Lajas in Puerto Rico said: "It is a huge accomplishment that someone from Puerto Rico and of Lajas descent has triumphed with such a high-ranking position."[61] Her success is not that of an individual, but of a tribe. Latino legal activists were quick to claim her nomination as something of their own. Cesar Perales of LatinoJustice PRLDEF proclaimed: "This is the most important Hispanic appointment that has been made in this country's history. It is a recognition that *we* are coming of age, that *we can be one of nine* wise people on the Supreme Court, making decisions that affect everyone in this country."[62]

Maria Hinojosa of PBS expressed a similar sentiment: "This nomination, like nothing before it, has made it clear that *we* finally exist as intellectual arbiters in *our* America. *We* exist as powerbrokers. It is a dynamic we are working hard to grasp and own and make real. Sotomayor has made it real for all of us."[63] Despite living in the first human civilization to have ended slavery and eliminated class barriers, Hinojosa was shocked to see a Latina nominated : "I was truly not expecting to hear the news and could scarcely believe it. Do we really have a *Puerto Rican woman from the South Bronx* nominated to serve on SCOTUS? Like they say on 'Saturday Night Live' -- Really? No! REALLY?"[64] And thus Sotomayor's race and gender are two of the most important topics of her nomination for those on both ends of the political spectrum. For better or for worse, Americans are attempting to discern what her ethnicity means to her and how it might impact her performance on the Supreme Court.

Sotomayor has made several alarming statements in regard to her minority status:

> "I would hope that a wise Latina woman with the richness of her experiences would more often than not reach a better conclusion than a white male who hasn't lived that life."[65]

"Whether born from experience or inherent physiological or cultural differences, our gender and national origins may and will make a difference in our judging."[66]

"Personal experiences affect the facts that judges choose to see."[67]

"I wonder whether by ignoring our differences as women or men of color we do a disservice both to the law and society."[68]

"Your childhood environment shapes your perceptions, your character, your sense of values... To the extent that I lived in an environment wrought with poverty and the mixture of responses to it, I had perhaps a much more complex understanding of human nature."[69]

"I willingly accept that we who judge must not deny the differences resulting from experience and heritage, but attempt, as the Supreme Court suggests, continuously to judge when those opinions, sympathies and prejudices are appropriate."[70]

Many have responded by terming Sotomayor a racist, noting she interprets the world and acts according to race. Her critics duly note that if a white man had made similar statements – "I would hope that a white man, with the richness of his experiences, would more often than not reach a better conclusion than a Latina or black woman who hasn't lived that life" – he would be castigated as a racist. The liberal response is that minorities, or former victims of racism, cannot themselves be racists because the power structure favors the white majority. This line of reasoning led Rush Limbaugh to term Sotomayor a "reverse racist":

> [Liberals] say that minorities cannot be racists because they don't have the power to implement their racism. Well, those days are gone, because

reverse racists certainly do have the power. ... Obama is the greatest living example of a reverse racist, and now he's appointed one.[71]

Former House Speaker Newt Gingrich joined in calling Sotomayor a racist, posting on twitter, "new racism is no better than old racism."[72]

Sotomayor's comments wouldn't be so bad if she simply stated her background and heritage inevitably would affect her perspective. Such a statement would not indicate any preference for one race over others, or intent to favor one over others. However, she goes much further by saying she *hopes* a Latina woman would judge "better" than a white male. Most Westerners aspire to equality. Sotomayor's statement aspires for one group – Hispanic females – to be better than another – white males. Her comment fits within theories of standpoint epistemology and other Marxist notions, which argue that members of socially marginalized groups are privileged with superior perspectives to those of the dominant members of society.

The concern for many Americans is that if Sotomayor feels she is or has been marginalized, and therefore believes she brings a superior perspective to the court, might she rule rather subjectively as a judge and feel perfectly justified in doing so? Will she punish people because of the color of their skin, their wealth or favorable upbringing? Will she self-righteously bring her bias to the court? Her words and actions have, at times, indicated some degree of resentment toward white people. While at Princeton, she co-chaired Acción Puertorriqueña, a Puerto Rican advocacy group on campus. She filed a formal complaint with the Department of Education, Health and Welfare accusing the university of discrimination in its hiring and admission processes. She wrote a brash article on the subject for *The Daily Princetonian*: "The facts imply and reflect a total absence of regard, concern and respect for an entire people and their culture... In effect, they represent an effort — a successful effort so far — to relegate an important cultural sector of the population to oblivion."[73]

Sotomayor's racial comments will be discussed at length during her confirmation. The underlying issue is her avowed empathy – an empathy Obama said he would look for in his nominees. The mixing of "empathy" and justice is a new ideal for American society. It represents a profound and uncertain departure from the past. Thomas Sowell writes,

> There is a reason why the statue of Justice wears a blindfold. There are things that courts are not supposed to see or recognize when making their decisions-- the race you belong to, whether you are rich or poor, and other personal things that could bias decisions by judges and juries.

> It is an ideal that a society strives for, even if particular judges or juries fall short of that ideal. Now, however, President Barack Obama has repudiated that ideal itself by saying

that he wants to appoint judges with
"empathy" for particular groups.[74]

Sowell points to Sotomayor's decision in
Ricci v. DeStefano as particularly dangerous.
She apparently felt empathy for the black
firefighters but not the white firefighters.
The decision is the subject of Ann Coulter's
May 27, 2009, column: "I feel your pain.
Not theirs. Yours."[75] Sowell says "that kind
of empathy would for all practical purposes
repeal the 14th Amendment to the
Constitution of the United States, which
guarantees 'equal protection of the laws' to
all Americans."[76]

But not all are so worried by the new
trend. Sotomayor's supporters ask, what's so
bad about empathy? Columnist Michael
Kinsley writes, "a lifetime appointment to
the Supreme Court is a special kind of job.
Nowhere is a bit of diversity more obviously
desirable. Nowhere is the case stronger for
taking race, ethnicity and gender into
account."[77] Following Sotomayor's
nomination, *Boston Globe* columnist Ellen
Goodman wrote, "I've never been sure why

Lady Justice wore a blindfold as part of her permanent wardrobe. Yes, it's supposed to be a symbol of impartiality. But it does limit her vision a bit." Goodman continues,

> The truth is that we want judges who 'get it.' The myth of justice as a matter of pure objective reasoning that could be meted out by a computer is just that, a myth. Check all those 5-4 decisions. Part of 'getting it,' says Susan Bandes, author of *Passions of the Law*, is 'the capacity to know what's at stake for all the litigants.' In short, empathy.

> Finally, as this debate goes on, it's worth asking what exactly would a judge without empathy look like? Bandes offers a name straight out of 'Star Trek': 'Spock.'

> Justice Spock? Science Fiction v. The Law? Remove your blindfolds.[78]

CNN's Gloria Borger echoes her thoughts: "how can anyone argue with the notion that who we are affects – in one way or another – how we view things? And on a collegial, multi-member court, isn't that diversity of experience a good thing?"[79] Similarly, author Caroline Presno says a justice's empathy adds to the court's objectivity:

> Empathy requires drawing on thoughts and feelings common to all humanity such as confusion, emptiness, joy, and hope. Even if it is not possible to relate to a specific event, it is possible to relate to some of the ideas, themes and emotions behind it. Empathizing in this way requires an objectivity and perceptiveness that is quite compatible with the rule of law.[80]

The argument is that Sotomayor's "empathy" is nothing more than a synonym for "diversity," though her detractors have construed it to mean she is a judicial activist. Borger notes that despite Sotomayor's long record, conservatives have failed to produce sufficient examples to prove her "empathy" translates to something negative:

> And then there's this: Can anyone point to a pattern in Sotomayor's opinions that are based more on 'empathy' than the law? Of course not.

> And that's precisely the point: Unless Sotomayor's opponents can succeed in using her judicial record to portray her as a passionate, wild-eyed judge who depends more on emotion more than legal precedent, they're in for a tough time.

> If they think empathy is a dirty word, they'll have to convince the American public.[81]

And what of Sotomayor's alleged racism? Clearly, her race plays a central role in her daily life and thought processes, perhaps to an excessive extent. However, her rulings do not indicate she's bent on retribution, or unjustly punishing white men from the bench. Even if she truly believes Latina women are physiologically and culturally superior to white men, the evidence suggests she is not the caricatured, Latina avenger some opponents portray her as. She sided against the white men in *Ricci,* but it was only one decision of many involving race. Tom Goldstein analyzed 50 of Sotomayor's roughly 100 cases dealing with discrimination charges. Sotomayor accepted the claims of racial discrimination in only 3 of the 50 cases.[82]

In the case *Pappas v. Giuliani*, the 2nd Circuit Court of Appeals ruled that the New York City Police Department was justified in firing Thomas Pappas for anonymously mailing racially offensive materials to political groups from his home. Pappas claimed the NYPD was infringing on his First Amendment rights. Sotomayor agreed with him, dissenting from her fellow judges. She said that although the materials were "patently offensive, hateful, and insulting," the majority was "gloss[ing] over three decades of jurisprudence and the centrality of First Amendment freedoms in our lives just because it is confronted with speech it does not like." Just as *Ricci* is trumpeted as proof that Sotomayor is too empathetic, *Pappas* could just as well be trumpeted as evidence she isn't empathetic enough. A legal realist, or judicial activist, would have been inclined to concur with the majority, saying the historic victimhood of particular minority groups justifies infringing on Pappas' First Amendment rights.

Obama mentor Charles Ogletree argues the public must look to Sotomayor's record as a judge rather than her few controversial comments:

> It is downright silly to suggest that two comments by a judge during a panel discussion and a speech somehow outweigh the thousands of cases that she's been involved [with in] 17 years. If you want to know a judge's judicial philosophy, read what they write and what they say as a judge.[83]

Some people agree diversity on the court is a good thing, but note that while Sotomayor adds diversity in some ways, she detracts in others. Sotomayor would make the sixth Catholic justice on the court. Though the United States is approximately 51% Protestant, 24% Catholic, and 1.7% Jewish, the Supreme Court is comprised of 6 Catholics, 2 Jews, and a single Protestant. The court also is skewed in geographic representation. 6 out of 9 justices are from the Northeast. The remaining are from Illinois, California, and Georgia. The Northeast represents about 17% of the U.S. population but fills 67% of the seats on the court.

The debate over Sotomayor's racism has already occurred once before. During her bruising confirmation process in 1998, questions were raised as to whether she could be impartial. Afterward, she reflected on the debate positively: "So long as people of good will are participating in the process and attempting to be balanced in their approach, then the system will remain healthy."[84] It remains to be seen whether the national debate will run its course positively a second time.

Intelligence: Brilliant Scholar or Piddling Intellect?

One of the most prominent debates following Sotomayor's nomination was whether she possessed the intellectual prowess to serve on the high court. Some regard her as highly intelligent, others dismiss her as a pompous dolt.

Her advocates include Rachel Moran, a former classmate at Yale, who says of Sotomayor: "She has a keen intellect, an articulate voice, and a sense of humor (though this is not usually mentioned in the press coverage). I think she will be a formidable presence on the Court... a lively, engaging, and challenging colleague for the other Justices."[85] Other former classmates have happily stepped forward to defend her intelligence in the *New York Times*, *Washington Post*, and other publications.[86]

Lawyers give her mixed reviews in their anonymous comments published in the

Almanac of the Federal Judiciary. Many are impressed:

> "She is frighteningly smart. She is intellectually tough."

> "She is very intelligent."

> "She is very good. She is bright."

> "She is very smart."

> "Her opinions are generally well-reasoned and well-argued."

> "She is a very good writer."

> "Her writing is not distinguished, but is perfectly competent."

Others, not so much:

> "She is a good judge, but not quite as smart as she thinks she is."

> "She is not [as] intellectual as some."

"I am not too impressed with her…
she doesn't always get the facts."

"She is temperamental and excitable.
She seems angry."

"She is overly aggressive--not very
judicial. She does not have a very
good temperament."

"She really lacks judicial
temperament. She behaves in an out
of control manner. She makes
inappropriate outbursts."[87]

Jeffrey Rosen of *The New Republic*
interviewed numerous Democrats who
formerly worked with Sotomayor as law
clerks or federal prosecutors in New York.
Many questioned "her ability to provide an
intellectual counterweight to the conservative
justices, as well as a clear liberal alternative."
A former law clerk said, "She has an inflated
opinion of herself, and is domineering during
oral arguments, but her questions aren't

penetrating and don't get to the heart of the issue." Another commented, "She's a fine Second Circuit judge--maybe not the smartest ever, but how often are Supreme Court nominees the smartest ever?" One interviewee supported Sotomayor, saying "I know the word on the street is that she's not the brainiest of people, but I didn't have that experience... She's an incredibly impressive person, she's not shy or apologetic about who she is, and that's great."[88]

At times, Sotomayor's colleagues wonder if she fully grasps what's going on around her. They say she has a tendency to get carried away, jumping to conclusions and then closing her mind to alternatives. During one argument, a judicial colleague leaned over to her and said, "Will you please stop talking and let them talk?" Rosen points to another questionable behavior:

> Sotomayor, several former clerks complained, rankled her colleagues by sending long memos that didn't distinguish between substantive and trivial points, with petty editing

suggestions--fixing typos and the like--rather than focusing on the core analytical issues.[89]

Sotomayor is doubted, in part, because the American system favors minorities. One of the unfortunate consequences of Affirmative Action is that it means minorities can never actually achieve anything without considerable doubt over their merit. Whatever success a Hispanic individual might have had in his own right is rendered unattainable. He can reach the top easier than before, but the public will always wonder if he really belongs there. Was he more qualified than everyone else, or was it simply a matter of his skin being darker? Did he earn his high position, or was he promoted by white guilt?

Everything Sotomayor has achieved is called into question because the system unequally favors her race and gender. Her proponents present her resume as proof of her aptitude, and it is undeniably impressive. She graduated Princeton with honors, was an editor for the Yale Law Journal, has occupied a seat on the federal bench for over a decade – and has accomplished all of this in spite of her Hispanic heritage and childhood poverty. Yet many Americans wonder whether her accomplishments were not in spite of, but *because of* her Hispanic heritage and childhood poverty. Did she really score better than fellow applicants to Princeton and Yale, or were the admissions counselors just glad to receive a minority student from the Projects? Should she have graduated with honors from Princeton, or were professors overly lenient along the way, grading her papers more favorably than those of white students? She was an editor of the Yale Law Journal, but even Barack Obama admitted to benefitting from affirmative action during his time as president of the Harvard Law Review. And as far as her judgeships, any politician would be delighted to be connected to her appointments. She has been "the first Hispanic" this or that at many points in her career. Democrats were thrilled to beat the Republicans to nominating the first Hispanic to the Supreme Court.

The strongest proof of Sotomayor's competence is her time in private practice with Pavia & Harcourt. She could not have succeeded in commercial litigation without genuinely grasping the law, quickly ascertaining its proper application in various scenarios, forming logical arguments and delivering them with skill. The midtown Manhattan firm would not have promoted her to partner if she failed to make them money. And given her high salaries, she clearly was bringing in a good amount. Clients were impressed. She got them results.

Many of the liberals who question Sotomayor's intelligence clarify that they are certain she is a smart woman. At issue is her lack of scholarly work. They would have preferred someone more professorial, an intellectual luminary with a noteworthy vision for the law. Jonathan Turley writes,

> My main concern is the lack of intellectual depth in her past opinions. Objecting to the intellectual content of opinions is not the same as objecting to the intellect of an individual. Smart

people can have little vision in the law or other fields. No one would suggest that Sotomayor is not incredibly bright. It is her legal vision and the depth of her legal philosophy that is at issue in confirmation debates.

… Looking objectively at the body of opinions by Judge Sotomayor, one is not overwhelmed by their depth. There is nothing in this body of work that would scream out for the elevation of the author to the Court.[90]

Still others say she might not be a Samuel Alito or John Roberts, but so what? Perhaps interpreting the Constitution needn't be left to the aristocrats. Columnist Craig Hixon writes,

Faithfully upholding the United States Constitution is not rocket surgery. In fact, I feel qualified. I'm not qualified to build a house, investigate a homicide, run a dairy farm, administer physical therapy, cook at a five-star restaurant (maybe a two-star), or cut hair. These jobs all require special skills and training. The Constitution is a simple document that you can read three times in an hour. It is much easier to know intricately the Constitution than any one of the Harry Potter novels. Even if you argue that our citizen jurists should also read the Federalist papers and an assortment of writings by the Founders, a significant number of folks could be up to speed in short order.[91]

But such discussion is irrelevant because the attacks on Sotomayor's intelligence don't match up to the reality of her accomplishments. She is not an average woman picked at random for the Supreme Court. She has excelled in both private practice and public service, gradually moving up the ranks to where she is today. Former Attorney General Alberto Gonzales told CNN Sotomayor is fit for the job: "A president is not required to nominate the most qualified person to the court. I think he's obliged to nominate someone who is well- qualified. And I think, by any measure, she is well-qualified."[92]

Another strong, opinionated woman was nominated for an important public position in August, 2008. She was younger than her colleagues and lacked the polished upbringing of New England elites. Her detractors immediately questioned her intelligence, labeling her a white trash ditz. Crude accusations of stupidity followed her for the duration of her campaign and beyond. Conservatives were right in arguing Sarah Palin couldn't possibly be the fool liberals made her out to be. She accomplished too much in her career, often with the odds against her, to be a person of inferior intelligence. Conservatives must accept the same argument for Sonia Sotomayor. Judge Sotomayor's successful career proves her above-average intelligence. Any charges to the contrary will look like racism and sexism – in some cases, rightfully so.

The Judicial Branch: Limited in Power, or True Source of Legislation?

One of the most incriminating videos of Sotomayor circulated after her nomination is one in which she tells a group of law students:

> …court of appeals is where policy is made. And I know — I know this is on tape, and I should never say that because we don't make law. I know. O.K. I know. I'm not promoting it. I'm not advocating it. I'm — you know.

The comment was made in 2005 during a panel discussion with students who were considering becoming law clerks. The brief excerpt made its rounds across the blogosphere, becoming an instant YouTube sensation. Although Sotomayor says "we don't make law," her mannerisms and tone suggest, "OK, yes, we do make law." She was caught revealing too much, immediately backpedalling, but also giving the students a sort of wink-and-nod. Conservatives circulated the video online as proof Sotomayor was a judicial activist.

The issue of where law is made is particularly relevant to conservatives because the nation's current laws on abortion are products of the Supreme Court. *Roe v. Wade* ended the democratic debate on abortion, overturning 46 states' laws addressing the matter. The decision should terrify every American regardless of his or her views of abortion. If the court can decree such legislation on one issue – abortion – it could just as well decree legislation on any other issue. The constitutional basis for abortion cited in *Roe,* as most liberal and conservative scholars agree, is nonexistent. The justices could just as easily find a constitutional basis for banning gay marriage.

Judicial activism is dangerous to liberals and conservatives alike because it kills the political process. It takes legislation approved by the people and replaces it with legislation approved by nine justices. The people are effectively disenfranchised. When congressmen act against the will of the people, they are voted out and their legislation is changed. When justices act against the will of the people, their legislation stands. They remain for life, or for as long as they wish, and their decisions stand regardless of public outcry. They are appointed, not elected, and so are not answerable to the people.

Roe v. Wade is generally invoked as a measure of one's support for abortion rights. Either one supports the decision and is pro-choice, or one opposes the decision and is pro-life. Actually, there is very little reason to support it whether one advocates for abortion rights or not. The decision reads like a bill out of Congress, creating a host of laws, regulations, and new terms like "trimester." It set a dangerous new precedent whereby judges could create law.

No serious legal scholar plays along with the notion that *Roe v. Wade* somehow fits within the Constitution. As Watergate prosecutor Archibald Cox said in 1976, "Neither historian, nor layman, nor lawyer will be persuaded that all the prescriptions of Justice Blackmun are part of the Constitution."[93] John Hart Ely, Alan Dershowitz, Justice John Paul Stevens, William Saletan, Cass Sunstein, Benjamin Wittes, Jeffrey Rosen, and Michael Kinsley – all are prominent, liberal intellectuals, and all have expressed disappointment in *Roe*. Even Edward Lazarus, a former Blackmun clerk, concedes: "As a matter of constitutional interpretation and judicial method, *Roe* borders on the indefensible. I say this as someone utterly committed to the right to choose."[94]

Both Republicans and Democrats should take pause when they hear a prospective Supreme Court Justice say the court "is where policy is made." Sotomayor will potentially serve on the Supreme Court for decades, her decisions affecting entire generations of Americans. Liberals might like her policies at first, but could be disappointed as time goes on. If they change their minds, or if Sotomayor changes hers, there is no recourse for removing her from her position of power. Imagine if Americans had been stuck with George W. Bush for life. He enjoyed approval ratings in the high 60s during his first months in office, but left with approval ratings in the low 30s. Over one-third of Americans changed their minds about George W. Bush. They acted on their change of opinion by voting against Bush's party in the 2006 and 2008 elections. No such process of review exists for Supreme Court justices. Fortunately, the Constitution confines justices to a very limited role, one in which they cannot make law.

All of that said, is Sonia Sotomayor a judicial activist? Is her widely circulated comment, quoted above, enough to prove that she fundamentally misunderstands the role of the judicial branch? Deborah O'Malley of the Heritage Foundation says yes: "Both her public statements and her attempt to smother the arguments of litigants she disfavors (such as in Ricci) reveal that she is no defender of the rule of law, but an unabashed hard-Left judicial activist."[95] Jonathan Turley issues an emphatic "No":

I cannot find any evidence to support the view that Sotomayor is an activist. Indeed, I cannot find much evidence to support the assumption by both ends of the spectrum that she is extremely liberal. She is clearly not as liberal as other short-list candidates like Diane Wood of the Seventh Circuit. She votes regularly with her conservative colleagues and does not have a blind voting record in areas like discrimination etc. If you compare her opinions to Justice Sam Alito when he was an appellate judge, she is the very personification of blind justice. Alito rarely voted against the government and was as predictable as a Swiss clock in terms of outcome in cases.[96]

As to the court's legislation in *Roe v. Wade*, Sotomayor has given very little indication as to where she stands on abortion. In 2007, Obama assured pro-choice groups that he "would not appoint somebody who doesn't believe in the right to privacy" (some scholars interpret the Constitution as suggesting a right to privacy, from which they derive a right to abortion).[97] Nonetheless, pro-choice advocates have expressed considerable doubt in Sotomayor's reliability. She has ruled only tangentially on abortion, and has not made any public statements on the case. Most people assume a liberal like Sotomayor, appointed by a liberal like Obama, would have to strongly support abortion rights and the court's previous legislation on the matter. Liberals could find themselves sorely disappointed, and conservatives pleasantly surprised.[98]

E.J. Dionne warns liberals they may be disappointed on other issues as well. Sotomayor might not be the radical individual they expected from Obama. He writes,

> ...even though they should support her confirmation, liberals would be foolish to embrace Sotomayor as one of their own because her record is clearly that of a moderate. It is highly unlikely that she will push the court to

the left. Indeed, on many issues of concern to business, she is likely to make the Chamber of Commerce perfectly happy.[99]

Sotomayor has dreamed of the Supreme Court for decades, and so has been extremely measured in her public comments. Other than a few controversial statements, she gives little indication of being a judicial activist. Her "empathy," thus far, has not resulted in a pattern of her legislating from the bench. Even on issues of racial discrimination, she has generally sided against the party claiming discrimination. She appears to follow the existing laws; not create new ones.

In Her Own Words

Sotomayor delivered the following address at the May 26, 2009, press conference in which President Obama announced her nomination:

"The president has said to you that I bring my family. In the audience is my brother Juan Sotomayor – he's a physician in Syracuse, New York; my sister-in-law, Tracy; my niece Kiley – she looks like me; my twin nephews, Conner and Corey.

"I stand on the shoulders of countless people, yet there is one extraordinary person who is my life aspiration. That person is my mother, Celina Sotomayor. My mother has devoted her life to my brother and me. And as the president mentioned, she worked often two jobs to help support us after dad died. I have often said that I am all I am because of her, and I am only half the woman she is.

"Sitting next to her is Omar Lopez, my mom's husband and a man whom I have grown to adore. I thank you for all that you have given me and continue to give me. I love you.

"I chose to be a lawyer and ultimately a judge because I find endless challenge in the complexities of the law. I firmly believe in the rule of law as the foundation for all of our basic rights.

"For as long as I can remember, I have been inspired by the achievement of our founding fathers. They set forth principles that have endured for than more two centuries. Those principles are as meaningful and relevant in each generation as the generation before. It would be a profound privilege for me to play a role in applying those principles to the questions and controversies we face today.

"Although I grew up in very modest and challenging circumstances, I consider my life to be immeasurably rich. I was raised in a

Bronx public housing project, but studied at two of the nation's finest universities.

"I did work as an assistant district attorney, prosecuting violent crimes that devastate our communities. But then I joined a private law firm and worked with international corporations doing business in the United States.

"I have had the privilege of serving as a federal district court trial judge, and am now serving as a federal appellate circuit court judge.

"This wealth of experiences, personal and professional, have helped me appreciate the variety of perspectives that present themselves in every case that I hear. It has helped me to understand, respect and respond to the concerns and arguments of all litigants who appear before me, as well as to the views of my colleagues on the bench.

"I strive never to forget the real world consequences of my decisions on individuals, businesses and government.

"It is a daunting feeling to be here. Eleven years ago, during my confirmation process for appointment to the Second Circuit, I was given a private tour of the White House. It was an overwhelming experience for a kid from the South Bronx. Yet, never in my wildest childhood imaginings did I ever envision that moment, let alone did I ever dream that I would live this moment.

"Mr. President, I greatly appreciate the honor you are giving me, and I look forward to working with the Senate in the confirmation process. I hope that as the Senate and American people learn more about me, they will see that I am an ordinary person who has been blessed with extraordinary opportunities and experiences. Today is one of those experiences.

"Thank you again, sir."

Notes

[1] Mike Shalin, "Attorney: Judge Sotomayor's simply Supreme," *Boston Herald*, 2 Apr 1995.

[2] Neil A. Lewis, "G.O.P., Its Eyes On High Court, Blocks a Judge," *The New York Times*, 13 Jun 1998.

[3] Larry Neumeister, "JUDGE LEARNS HUMILITY FROM GROWING UP IN HOUSING PROJECT>CHILDHOOD SHAPED JUDGE'S CHARACTER, VALUES, PERCEPTIONS," *The Journal Star* (Peoria, IL), 22 Nov 1998.

[4] See, e.g. Jena Heath, "Hot issues may affect Gonzales' future," *Austin American-Statesman*, 9 Dec 2001; Michael McGough, "ELECTION LIKELY TO ALTER MAKE-UP OF TOP COURT," *Pittsburgh Post-Gazette* (PA), 9 Aug 2004.

[5] David Lightman, "Obama court pick likely to be OK'd," *The Sun News* (Myrtle Beach, SC), 1 May 2009.

[6] CNN, "Source: Obama's pick wasn't pegged to Scalia," 27 May 2009 <http://politicalticker.blogs.cnn.com/2009/05/27/source-obamas-pick-wasnt-pegged-to-scalia/>.

[7] ALEXANDER BURNS and JOSH GERSTEIN, "White House to Sonia Sotomayor critics: Be 'careful'," Politico, 27 May 2009 <http://www.politico.com/news/stories/0509/23016.html>.

[8] Arianna Huffington, "Why Sotomayor's Confirmation Debate Is the D.C. Equivalent of Rock of Love," Huffington Post, 28 May 2009 <http://www.huffingtonpost.com/arianna-huffington/why-sotomayors-confirmati_b_208863.html>.

[9] Charles Krauthammer, "Sotomayor: Rebut, Then Confirm," *Washington Post*, 29 May 2009.

[10] Danica Coto, "Sotomayor maintains Puerto Rican roots," AP, 26 May 2009; and David G. Savage, "Court Rises as Campaign Issue," *St. Paul Pioneer Press* (MN), 26 Oct 2004.

[11] "Hispanic Woman Would Be First on Federal Bench," *The San Francisco Chronicle*, 1 Jun 1992.

[12] AP, "Woman to judge baseball issues," *San Antonio Express-News*, 28 Mar 1995.

[13] Neil A. Lewis, "On a Supreme Court Prospect's Résumé: 'Baseball Savior'," *The New York Times,* 15 May 2009.

[14] Jan Hoffman, "A Breakthrough Judge: What She Always Wanted," *The New York Times*, 25 Sep 1992.

[15] Larry Neumeister, "Woman rises from slums to U.S. 2nd Circuit Court of Appeals," *Fort Worth Star-Telegram*, 29 Nov 1998.

[16] Jan Hoffman, "A Breakthrough Judge: What She Always Wanted," *The New York Times*, 25 Sep 1992.

[17] Larry Neumeister, "Woman rises from slums to U.S. 2nd Circuit Court of Appeals," *Fort Worth Star-Telegram*, 29 Nov 1998.

[18] Amy Goldstein and Jerry Markon, "Heritage Shapes Judge's Perspective," *Washington Post*, 27 May 2009.

[19] Neil A. Lewis, "On a Supreme Court Prospect's Résumé: 'Baseball Savior'," *The New York Times,* 15 May 2009.

[20] Amy Goldstein and Jerry Markon, "Heritage Shapes Judge's Perspective," *Washington Post*, 27 May 2009.

[21] Ibid.

[22] Jan Hoffman, "A Breakthrough Judge: What She Always Wanted," *The New York Times*, 25 Sep 1992.

[23] Stuart Auerbach, "Law Firm Apologizes to Yale Student," *The Washington Post*, 16 Dec 1978.

[24] Neil A. Lewis, "On a Supreme Court Prospect's Résumé: 'Baseball Savior'," *The New York Times,* 15 May 2009.

[25] Amy Goldstein and Jerry Markon, "Heritage Shapes Judge's Perspective," *Washington Post*, 27 May 2009.

[26] Jan Hoffman, "A Breakthrough Judge: What She Always Wanted," *The New York Times*, 25 Sep 1992.

[27] "Hispanic Woman Would Be First on Federal Bench," *The San Francisco Chronicle*, 1 Jun 1992.

[28] Neil A. Lewis, "On a Supreme Court Prospect's Résumé: 'Baseball Savior'," *The New York Times,* 15 May 2009.

[29] AP, "Woman to judge baseball issues," *San Antonio Express-News*, 28 Mar 1995.

[30] "Hispanic Woman Would Be First on Federal Bench," *The San Francisco Chronicle*, 1 Jun 1992.

[31] AP, "Woman to judge baseball issues," *San Antonio Express-News*, 28 Mar 1995.

[32] Ibid.

[33] Ibid.

[34] Ronald Blum, "Hearing, proposal could end strike," *Austin American-Statesmen*, 28 Mar 1995.

[35] AP, "FRIDAY HEARING SET IN BASEBALL STRIKE FEDERAL JUDGE ASKS OWNERS AND NLRB TO SUBMIT BRIEFS AND HOLDS OUT POSSIBILITY OF A QUICK RULING," *Rocky Mountain News*, 28 Mar 1995.

[36] Jerome Holtzman, "JUDGE HOLDS THE KEY," *Chicago Tribune*, 30 Mar 1995.

[37] "CLINTON URGES OWNERS: LET PLAYERS PLAY BALL," *Chicago Tribune*, 30 Mar 1995.

[38] Michael O'Connor, "Judge calls 'em as she sees 'em," *Boston Herald*, 31 Mar 1995.

[39] James C. McKinley, Jr. "Judge lives up to image," *Fort Worth Star-Telegram*, 1 Apr 1995.

[40] Jerome Holtzman and Andrew Bagnato, "STRIKE ENDS, DISPUTE DOESN'T," *Chicago Tribune*, 1 Apr 1995.

[41] AP, "Owners strike out once again," *San Antonio Express-News*, 12 May 1995.

[42] Mike Shalin, "Attorney: Judge Sotomayor's simply Supreme," *Boston Herald*, 2 Apr 1995.

[43] Furman Bisher, "No place for judge to learn baseball," *The Atlanta Journal and The Atlanta Constitution*, 1 Apr 1995.

[44] Dave Van Dyck, "Unhappy Owners Can't Escape The Feeling They're in a Corner," *Chicago Sun-Times*, 2 Apr 1995.

[45] Robert Marchant, "Clinic's closing brings relief," *The Journal News* (Westchester County, NY), 9 May 2002.

[46] "PUBLISHERS WIN RULING ON FREE-LANCE WRITERS," *The Buffalo News,* 14 Aug 1997.

[47] Benny Evangelista, "Free-Lance Writers Win Electronic Victory," *The San Francisco Chronicle*, 28 Sep 1999.

[48] Verena Dobnik, "JUDGE RULES REAL WORK MERITS REAL PAY," *The Record* (NJ), 20 Mar 1998.

[49] AP, "HOMELESS COLLECT PAY AFTER LAWSUIT \ DOZENS IN NEW YORK PICK UP LONG-OVERDUE CHECKS," *Akron Beacon Journal* (OH), 27 Oct 2000.

[50] "Judge finally received approval for nomination," *The Orlando Sentinel*, 3 Oct 1998.

[51] For further discussion of Ricci v. DeStefano, see Stuart Taylor, "Sotomayor And 'Disparate Impact'," *National Journal Magazine*, 30 May 2009.

[52] Eugene Robinson, "Grasping at Straws," RealClearPolitics, 29 May 2009 <http://www.realclearpolitics.com/articles/2009/05/29/grasping_at_straws_96714.html>.

[53] AP, "DYSLEXIC WOMAN WINS BAR EXAM SUIT," *The Record* (New Jersey), 17 Aug 2001.

[54] 304 F3d 183 Center for Reproductive Law and Policy v. W Bush

[55] Frank J. Murray, "Appeals court upholds 'perp walks' - Cites possible deterrent effect," *The Washington Times*, 11 Sep 2003.

[56] Richard Simon, "Court overturns Bush rule on air conditioners," *Duluth News-Tribune* (MN), 14 Jan 2004.

[57] ARIELLE LEVIN BECKER, "COURT LOOKS AT INTERNET LIMITS," *The Hartford Courant*, 5 Mar 2008.

[58] Steve Collins, "Sotomayor had key role in Doninger case," *The Herald* (New Britain, CT), 28 May 2009.

[59] Mark Sherman, "First Hispanic justice? Some say it was Cardozo," AP, 26 May 2009.

[60] Jan Hoffman, "A Breakthrough Judge: What She Always Wanted," *The New York Times*, 25 Sep 1992.

[61] Danica Coto, "Sotomayor maintains Puerto Rican roots," AP, 26 May 2009.

[62] Michael A. Fletcher, "Latino Legal Activists Hail Sotomayor Choice," *The Washington Post*, 26 May 2009 <http://voices.washingtonpost.com/44/2009/05/26/latino_legal_activists_hail_so.html>, emphasis added.

[63] Maria Hinojosa, "A Supreme Sotomayor: How My Country Has Caught Up to Me," Huffington Post, 29 May 2009 <http://www.huffingtonpost.com/maria-hinojosa/a-

supreme-sotomayor-how-m_b_209185.html>, emphasis added.

[64] Ibid.

[65] Charlie Savage, "A Judge's View of Judging Is on the Record," *The New York Times*, 15 May 2009.

[66] Ibid.

[67] Ibid.

[68] Ibid.

[69] Larry Neumeister, "JUDGE LEARNS HUMILITY FROM GROWING UP IN HOUSING PROJECT>CHILDHOOD SHAPED JUDGE'S CHARACTER, VALUES, PERCEPTIONS," *The Journal Star* (Peoria, IL), 22 Nov 1998.

[70] Ben Feller, "Obama sure Sotomayor would restate 2001 comment," AP, 29 May 2009.

[71] Andy Barr, "Rush Limbaugh: Sonia Sotomayor a 'reverse racist,' 'hack'," Politico, 26 May 2009 <http://www.politico.com/news/stories/0509/22983.html>.

[72] "White House Smacks Gingrich For Calling Sotomayor A Racist," Huffington Post, 27 May 2009 <http://www.huffingtonpost.com/2009/05/27/white-house-admonishes-gi_n_208227.html>.

[73] Sheryl Gay Stolberg, "Sotomayor, a Trailblazer and a Dreamer," *The New York Times*, 26 May 2009.

[74] Thomas Sowell, "The Statue of Justice Wears a Blindfold," RealClearPolitics, 7 May 2009, accessed 29 May 2009 <http://www.realclearpolitics.com/articles/2009/05/07/emp athy_versus_law_part_iii_96334.html>.

[75] Ann Coulter, "I FEEL YOUR PAIN. NOT THEIRS. YOURS." 27 May 2009.

[76] Thomas Sowell, "'Empathy' in Action," RealClearPolitics, 27 May 2009 <http://www.realclearpolitics.com/articles/2009/05/27/emp athy_in_action_96681.html>

[77] Michael Kinsley, "The Right's Court Complex," *The Washington Post*, 29 May 2009.

[78] Ellen Goodman, "WHY FEAR EMPATHY ON SUPREME COURT?," *San Jose Mercury News*, 22 May 2009.

[79] Gloria Borger, "'Empathy' not a dirty word for a judge," CNN, 28 May 2009 <http://www.cnn.com/2009/POLITICS/05/28/borger.soto mayor/index.html>.

[80] Caroline Presno, "Karl Rove Needs a Dictionary: Get Your Definition of Empathy Correct," Huffington Post, 29 May 2009 <http://www.huffingtonpost.com/caroline-presno/karl-rove-needs-a-diction_b_209016.html>.

[81] Gloria Borger, "'Empathy' not a dirty word for a judge," CNN, 28 May 2009 <http://www.cnn.com/2009/POLITICS/05/28/borger.soto mayor/index.html>.

[82] Tom Goldstein, "Judge Sotomayor and Race," SCOTUSBlog, 29 May 2009 <http://www.scotusblog.com/wp/judge-sotomayor-and-race/>.

[83] Cynthia Gordy, "Obama's Mentor and Legal Scholar Weighs in on Supreme Court Nomination," *Essence*, 28 May 2009.

[84] Larry Neumeister, "JUDGE LEARNS HUMILITY FROM GROWING UP IN HOUSING PROJECT>CHILDHOOD SHAPED JUDGE'S CHARACTER, VALUES, PERCEPTIONS," *The Journal Star* (Peoria, IL), 22 Nov 1998.

[85] Bella DePaulo, "More about Sonia Sotomayor, From Someone Who Knew Her at Yale," Huffington Post, 26 May 2009 <http://www.huffingtonpost.com/bella-depaulo/more-about-sonia-sotomayo_b_207937.html>.

[86] See, e.g., Sheryl Gay Stolberg, "Sotomayor, a Trailblazer and a Dreamer," *The New York Times*, 26 May 2009.

[87] Harry Enten and Mark Murray, "Lawyers give Sotomayor mixed reviews," MSNBC, 26 May 2009 <http://firstread.msnbc.msn.com/archive/2009/05/26/1943705.aspx>

[88] Jeffrey Rosen, "The Case Against Sotomayor," *The New Republic,* 4 May 2009.

[89] Jeffrey Rosen, "The Case Against Sotomayor," *The New Republic,* 4 May 2009.

[90] Jonathan Turley, "President Picks Sonia Sotomayor," JonathanTurley.org, 26 May 2009, accessed 29 May 2009 <http://jonathanturley.org/2009/05/26/white-house-to-announce-court-pick-at-10-am/>.

[91] Craig Hixon, "Sonia Sotomayor and Judicial Intelligence," OpinionEditorials.com, 30 May 2009 <http://www.opinioneditorials.com/freedomwriters/chixon_20090530.html>.

[92] Wolf Blitzer, The Situation Room, CNN, 26 May 2009.

[93] Archibald Cox, The Role of the Supreme Court in American Government, 113–114 (Oxford U. Press 1976).

[94] Edward Lazarus, "The Lingering Problems with Roe v. Wade, and Why the Recent Senate Hearings on Michael McConnell's Nomination Only Underlined Them", Findlaw's Writ, 3 Oct 2002, accessed 25 May 2009 <http://writ.corporate.findlaw.com/lazarus/20021003.html>.

[95] Deborah O'Malley, "Sotomayor Doesn't Live Up to Obama's Word," RealClearPolitics, 29 May 2009 <http://www.realclearpolitics.com/articles/2009/05/29/sotomayor_doesnt_live_up_to_obamas_word_96725.html>.

[96] Jonathan Turley, "Confirming Nonsense: Both Liberals and Conservatives Distort Debate Over Sotomayor," JonathanTurley.org, 28 May 2009 <http://jonathanturley.org/2009/05/28/confirming-nonsense-both-liberals-and-conservatives-distort-debate-over-sotomayor>.

[97] Robert Barnes and Michael D. Shear, "Abortion Rights Backers Get Reassurances on Nominee," *Washington Post*, 29 May 2009.

[98] For more discussion on Sotomayor as a "stealth candidate," see Charlie Savage, "On Sotomayor, Some Abortion Rights Backers Are Uneasy," *The New York Times*, 27 May 2009.

[99] E.J. Dionne, "Sotomayor Is No Leftist," RealClearPolitics, 28 May 2009 <http://www.realclearpolitics.com/articles/2009/05/28/sotomayor_is_no_leftist_96696.html>.